Defense Security Service
Stakeholder Report 2012

Photo: The new Defense Adjudication Activities Facility located on Fort George G. Meade, Maryland. The building is the new home of the Defense Industrial Security Clearance Office.

I am pleased to present our annual Stakeholder Report. I think this issue is our best yet.

I arrived at DSS in December 2010 just as we were putting the final touches on last year's report. By the time this document is published, I will have marked my first year as Director. Therefore, this report is not only a review of DSS achievements in the past year, it is also a reflection of the first year of my tenure.

One of my priorities when I arrived at DSS was to renew and reinvigorate the strong partnership between DSS and industry. I committed myself and the agency to an open, transparent environment, to industry's success, and the success of the National Industrial Security Program. We have been successful, as you'll see in the concrete steps and actions documented here.

Last year's report included an ambitious list of priorities for FY11. I'm pleased to report we achieved many of our goals, we made great progress on others, and some remain works in progress. This year's report revisits the priorities of FY11 and chronicles our progress.

I'm very proud of the men and women at DSS and what we have been able to achieve. We have an exciting, unique mission at DSS and I have found serving as DSS Director to be a challenging, but gratifying experience. I hope you share my enthusiasm and I encourage you to learn more about DSS as you read further in this year's report.

Stanley L. Sims
Director

DSS Achievements

At the conclusion of the 2011 Stakeholder Report, DSS committed to enhancing and expanding its oversight of the National Industrial Security Program (NISP) and to reinvigorating the Security Education, Training and Awareness Program. The report also contained a list of 11 priorities for the coming year. The following pages list those priorities and the success DSS has demonstrated in meeting them. In some cases, work remains to be done before the agency can claim success. What DSS can claim however, is evidence of a committed, focused workforce dedicated to the success of its mission and the inclusion of its values in all activities.

FY11 Priority:

Renew and strengthen the partnership between Government and Industry Stakeholders for the betterment of national security in this evolving security environment.

DSS initiated an aggressive outreach program during the last year to better communicate with its Government and Industry Stakeholders. This was done in a spirit of cooperation and to ensure that DSS actions were open and transparent.

Outreach to Industry

The relationship between DSS and cleared industry is unique and built on a foundation of shared information and commitment to the protection of national security. To further strengthen this relationship and facilitate the effective and efficient sharing of information, DSS conducted an aggressive outreach program to industry. These events are held outside the normal assessment process and are designed to exchange information of interest and offer in-depth briefings on key initiatives.

Partnership with Industry (PWI)

DSS initiated the Partnership with Industry Program in 2009 when DSS and Lockheed Martin each exchanged a security professional for one week. The exchanges are governed by a Memorandum of Understanding (MOU) between DSS and the participating company, and are designed to allow participants to 'walk in each other's shoes' and see how the other side does business. The goal is improved communication and an enhanced understanding of DSS's oversight mission for the NISP. In addition, the program promotes skill development and is a useful tool to facilitate discussions of real-life industrial security concerns.

Today, there are six active industry participants and more than 26 cleared defense contractors have inquired about participation in the program, and DSS completed its sixth exchange this year.

Since its inception, 11 Industrial Security Representatives and two Information System Security Professionals from four regions and Headquarters have participated in the program. Thirteen Industry participants have come from across the United States – New Jersey, Colorado, Texas, Georgia, Arizona, New York, Virginia, Florida – and have worked in each of the four DSS regions.

The MOU determines which region can host an industry representative and restricts DSS from assigning DSS employees to a facility under their cognizance, unless required by operational necessity.

"My experience at the DSS Phoenix Field Office provided me with great insight into the day-to-day operations of DSS and their tremendous workload. I believe it will enhance my security skill level in that I will now be able to look at issues from a different perspective. I was also able to obtain information that we will be able to use to hopefully eliminate SSP (system security plan) rejections and possibly decrease the approval time, as well as improve our self-inspection process, and increase security awareness among our employees. I have also acquired numerous contacts within the Security community to rely on whenever questions arise."

"This was a great experience. I was able to see Industrial Security from another perspective. My focus going back will be to do a better job preparing for the "Team Reviews" on a continuous basis not just in getting ready for the audit. Each person I talked to answered questions and provided insight on their area of expertise."

"What I liked most about this program was the experience to closely work with Industry while witnessing firsthand how security plays a vital role in their organization. I had an opportunity to spend one week at a facility in Denver. During this period, I witnessed the facility's intention to fully comply with the requirements of the NISP, at times with intent to go above and beyond. To this facility, it's not just complying with the NISP, but also protecting their technology, their investment, and most importantly protecting national security."

Monthly Newsletter to Industry

In October 2010, DSS Field Operations conducted a customer satisfaction survey of NISP industry participants. This survey resulted in productive and value-added suggestions for improving the exchange of information and relationship between DSS and its industry partners. In response to these suggestions, Field Operations initiated a monthly email newsletter to inform Facility Security Officers (FSOs) of pertinent security related information such as recent policy, education and information updates. Since its inception, the newsletter has been distributed in a monthly email to all 13,000 plus cleared facilities. Feedback continues to be positive and very well received.

Support for Local Industry Events

During the past year, each DSS regional office supported local security meetings from Los Angeles, to Oklahoma, Hawaii and Virginia. In each case, DSS personnel were able to interact with industry personnel to share information, answer questions and introduce initiatives. In some cases, the audiences included more than 500 security professionals, while others were limited to 20 or 30 personnel.

The following is a list of some of the events DSS supported in the past year:

- The Virginia Beach Field Office briefed approximately 30 government and contractor personnel at a meeting of the Carolina Region of Industrial Security Professionals.

- The Atlanta Field Office hosted an Industrial Security Workshop for approximately 150 Facility Security Officers from northwest Florida, northern Alabama, Georgia and southwestern Mississippi.

- The Crystal City Field Office hosted the Quantico-area Industrial Security Awareness Council which has grown from just a few contractors to over 80 at the last meeting.

- The Huntsville Field Office participated in the NCMS Mid-South Chapter 12 annual training seminar in Huntsville, Ala., attended by approximately 225 security professionals from the local and surrounding community. The DSS Director also spoke at this event.

- The Irving and San Antonio Field Offices supported the annual Dallas-Fort Worth National Classification Management Society/Joint Security Awareness Council Conference attended by approximately 150 security professionals.

- The Maryland Field Office attended the 5th annual Central Maryland Industrial Security Advisory Committee Seminar and met with approximately 250 industry representatives.

- DSS field personnel have also attended and participated in Facility Security Officer (FSO) conferences at a number of cleared contractors. These events allow companies with multiple cleared locations to bring in a dispersed security staff and deliver a cohesive security message.

- The Honolulu Field Office supported a meeting of the Aloha Industrial Security Awareness Council, which was attended by 80 security professionals.

Government Outreach

DSS continues to sponsor venues that allow all government partners in industrial security to come together to meet, discuss and share issues of common concern. The objective is to provide a training opportunity for participants to gain a better understanding of the industrial security business. The meetings of the past year focused on Foreign Ownership Control and Influence (FOCI) and related activities. The topic was timely given the complexity of the issues and the increasing globalization across Defense Industry.

The two DSS Stakeholder Meetings held during the year both featured in depth presentations on FOCI, support to the Committee on Foreign Investment in the United States (CFIUS) process, FOCI procedures, and how the FOCI and CFIUS processes are related. National Interest Determinations (NID) and how they relate to the CFIUS and FOCI processes were also discussed in detail.

The Government Industrial Security Working Group (GISWG) had three meetings this year, all focused on the NID process. The meetings facilitated dialogue among the NID providers as each attendee shared their processes and best practices. DSS posted the Department of Energy, Office of the Director for National Intelligence and National Security Agency NID request check sheets on its website for all government contracting activities to review and use. DSS also used the meetings to share information on emerging and changing policies pertaining to FOCI and NIDs.

This year, DSS became a formal member of the Defense Criminal Investigative Organization Enterprise-wide Working Group (DEW Group). The Dew Group was created in 1997 to examine the best business practices of the Defense Criminal Investigative Organizations (DCIOs) with the goal of achieving enterprise-wide reforms and streamlining DCIO criminal and counterintelligence investigative resources and functions. DSS has participated for several years, but was not a charter member because it did not conduct the spectrum of investigative missions and did not have the same authorities as the DCIOs. DSS was made a charter member as a result of the value added by the CI Directorate, despite not having the same investigative authorities as the other members.

In addition to headquarters activities, a number of field offices participated in local government meetings and events. The Huntsville Field Office participated in the Northern Alabama CI Working Group Meeting with the FBI, Missile Defense Agency, 902nd MI (U.S. Army), and the Space and Missile Defense Command.

The staff of the Center for the Development of Security Excellence participated in a Staff Assistance Visit of another Defense agency where they shared their expertise and reviewed the agency's security practices.

The Irving Field Office met with representatives from a number of contracting activities at Tinker Air Force Base, Oklahoma.

FOCI Meetings

Oversight of companies under Foreign Ownership Control or Influence (FOCI) presents unique challenges to DSS. To increase awareness on these possible challenges, DSS hosted the 15th annual FOCI conference to provide updates on the latest developments in policy and procedures which affect companies operating with a FOCI mitigation plan. In attendance were approximately 180 Outside Directors and Proxy Holders, including former members of congress, ambassadors, service chiefs of staff, and departmental secretaries. Outside Directors and Proxy Holders serve in a pivotal role in ensuring FOCI companies implement all needed procedures and organizational changes pertaining to the security and safeguarding of classified and expert controlled information.

This session was followed by a conference for the Facility Security Officers (FSOs) from FOCI companies. Approximately 170 FSOs attended and learned about key policy and procedure updates. The FSO's were able to ask detailed FOCI questions to help them better protect the classified information at their facilities.

DSS has also initiated a number of smaller, more focused meetings with Outside Directors and Proxy Holders. Outside Directors and Proxy Holders exercise management prerogatives relating to the FOCI company in a way that ensures that the foreign shareholder can be effectively insulated from the undue influence of the cleared company. The first such meeting included five Outside Directors and Proxy Holders, and focused on FOCI policies and procedures. The meeting provided an opportunity for DSS to seek periodic feedback from a small, rotating membership of personnel.

Congressional Outreach

During the past year, DSS, through its Office of Legislative Affairs (OLA), hosted Congressional outreach events across the country to include Ohio, Massachusetts, Virginia, Maryland and California. The events were attended by 61 Congressional staffers.

In each case, the staffers received an overview of DSS operations from senior DSS personnel which focused on issues relevant to inquiries congressional offices commonly receive from constituents. DSS received and responded to over 500 inquiries from congressional offices this year related to clearance issues alone.

DSS OLA worked closely with their legislative affairs counterparts at the FBI to sponsor a joint outreach event for congressional staff at Marine Corps Base Quantico, the new location for DSS Headquarters. The coordinated program included a detailed briefing on identifying and preventing insider threats relating to corporate and government espionage in the Maryland and Virginia regions. The highly successful event increased the FBI's awareness of DSS's mission and achievements and established the framework for an ongoing partnership with the FBI for future joint Congressional events.

FY11 Priority:
Continue to provide support to the cleared defense industrial base to ensure it is effective in detecting and mitigating threats

As the DoD Cognizant Security Office for industrial security, DSS manages and administers the DoD portion of the National Industrial Security Program (NISP) for the DoD Components and other U.S. Government departments and agencies. Included in its oversight duties is responsibility for more than 13,000 cleared facilities. Not only is DSS responsible for ensuring that these facilities comply with the National Industrial Security Program Operating Manual (NISPOM), it is also dedicated to providing assistance to cleared contractor facilities and assisting management and Facility Security Officers in ensuring the protection of U.S. and foreign classified information and technologies. By ensuring the success of the NISP in industry, DSS supports national security and the warfighter. The following are examples of the DSS commitment to the NISP and its effective oversight.

MOA for Command Cyber Readiness Inspections (CCRI)

All facilities cleared under the NISP are subject to security reviews and assessments by DSS. NISP contractors that have connections to the Defense Information Systems Networks Secret Internet Protocol Router Network (SIPRNet) are subject to a compliance review by the Defense Information Systems Agency (DISA). In some cases, the same contractor facility would host two separate visits from two separate government agencies using different guidelines within weeks of one another. Contractor operations were disrupted and the separate reviews required dedicated resources to accommodate the visits.

DISA and DSS signed a Memorandum of Agreement (MOA) that defines the roles, responsibilities, and relationships between DISA and DSS for contractor classified information systems connecting to the SIPRNet. The MOA establishes DSS review teams, trained by DISA, to conduct Command Cyber Readiness Inspections (CCRI), at cleared contractor locations where DSS has oversight responsibility. The teaming arrangement presents a unified DoD face to cleared contractors.

DSS began implementation of the DISA CCRI program with focused training to include new terminology and assessment protocols for DSS Information System Security Professionals and Industrial Security Representatives. The first CCRI training session was held in October at DSS Headquarters at Quantico, Va.

There will also be an annual requirement for refresher training to keep DSS personnel up to date on the latest security issues and/or any new CCRI requirements.

The benefits of the MOA extend to both government and industry. For cleared industry, the MOA means one government visit and one face to industry. For the government it means making the best use of technically trained resources.

DSS will be scheduled for reviews by U.S. Cyber Command once DSS teams have been trained and certified.

The DSS Counterintelligence (CI) Directorate has published the document, *Targeting U.S. Technologies: A Trend Analysis of Reporting from Defense Industry*, for several years. The report is based on information obtained from DSS outreach and partnerships with stakeholders and customers, and includes the agency's analysis of suspicious contact reports received from cleared industry. It is designed to help cleared industry understand the nature of the threats they face and identify and recognize the techniques foreign collectors employ in their efforts to improperly acquire U.S. technologies.

In an effort to increase industry awareness and provide relevant, timely threat information, DSS CI has launched a number of new threat awareness and analysis products.

The Crimson Shield is a classified monthly snapshot of significant CI, intelligence, and security-related issues relevant to the cleared contractor community. It is meant to inform readers about attempts to compromise, exploit, and/or illegally acquire critical U.S. information and technology resident within cleared industry. Distribution includes the law enforcement/counterintelligence community as well as cleared contractors and national decision makers.

The Scarlet Sentinel is a quarterly unclassified report created to increase the knowledge and understanding of the nature and scope of vulnerabilities and threats to cleared industry. The purpose of the product is to educate readers about technology concerns and issues that facilitate the exploitation, compromise, or the illegal acquisition of critical U.S. information and technology. The product is also meant to inform readers of technology research, development, and acquisitions worldwide.

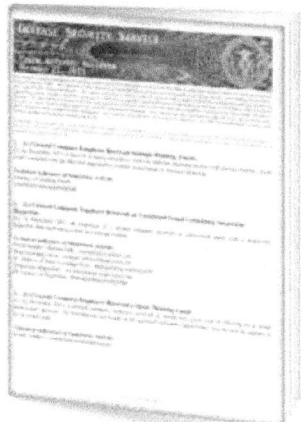

The Cyber Activity Bulletin is a bi-weekly unclassified summary containing information derived from cyber reports provided to DSS by contractors cleared under the NISP. The summaries included in this report are for official purposes and provided to facilitate a greater understanding of the nature and scope of cyber threats.

The Gray Torch is an individual company-focused report designed to strengthen the company's understanding of the nature of the foreign intelligence threat and to identify and recognize unlawful attempts to acquire U.S. technology developed or produced in the facilities operating under the NISP. Because of the proprietary information contained in these assessments, distribution is limited to the company that is the subject of the assessment. To date, 17 company assessments have been completed.

"DSS provided us with actionable intelligence."

"I want to thank you for all of the hard work that went into analyzing our information and building the report. We are all anxious to read the full briefing now! I am already working on a plan to have DSS present the briefing at our annual Security Managers conference in 2012."

"I regularly attend briefings provided by DIA and other DoD elements and was prepared to be 'underwhelmed' by DSS CI's presentation - however, I most certainly was not."

Quality Evaluation Program

During 2011, the Quality Assurance Office in Field Operations initiated new quality work product evaluation programs. The programs facilitate monthly reviews of work products for quality, consistency, and timeliness.

Peer and regional reviewers use evaluation criteria to review a sampling of security assessment reports and security vulnerability actions to ensure quality and compliance with requirements. The results are then shared with the Quality Assurance Office.

The Quality Assurance Office does a national roll-up of data to look for trends and process improvement. Trends have shown an overall improvement with quality of the reports since instituting the evaluation program. In general, the process identified a need to appropriately document assessment ratings and to adequately document internal communication when processing security violations and vulnerabilities. As a result, these trends drove process changes within field operations, i.e. new rating process and a revamped internal security violation process. The evaluation program also increased the sharing of best practices and information between offices, addressed areas in need of field guidance clarification and has improved the overall quality of DSS internal work products.

New ODAA Process Manual

The Office of the Designated Approving Authority (ODAA) is responsible for certification and accreditation (C&A) and oversight and management of cleared contractor's collateral classified computer systems. While the NISPOM provides the foundation for the review of all contractor security plans and the associated accreditations, DSS and industry interpretations of NISPOM requirements can be inconsistent. These inconsistencies negatively affected the security posture of accredited information systems across the country and in some cases, delayed system certification.

To address these inconsistencies, in June 2011, DSS introduced the Process Manual (Version 3.0) which introduces a new baseline security configuration as well as recommended templates. Use of the templates helps ensure all NISPOM requirements are addressed with the ultimate goal of improving the accuracy and consistency of information system technical configurations. Since the introduction of the manual, industry information systems security processes across the country have dramatically improved. Standards are better understood and systems are consistently configured in accordance with NISPOM requirements.

Expanded FSO Training

Under the National Industrial Security Program, FSOs at cleared facilities are required to complete security training. CDSE has long provided FSO training – an instructor-led, three-day course – noted for its long waiting lists for attendance. In 2007, CDSE began an initiative to transition this course to a web-based FSO curriculum, initially offering six online courses for facilities which possessed classified information and two online courses for non-possessing facilities.

Since the initial course offering the program has expanded to two curriculum tracks which provides 12 courses for non-possessing facilities and 16 courses for possessing facilities. The training covers such topics as the FSO Role in the NISP, facility clearances, personnel clearances, CI and threat awareness integration, derivative classification, marking, information security, security education, safeguarding and transmission of classified information, Industrial Security Facilities Database, reporting requirements, self-inspections, and visits and meetings.

A basic course in FOCI was recently added to both curriculum tracks and defines FOCI terms and processes as they relate to the NISP.

In FY11, there were more than 39,000 course completions, to include both instructor-led and web-based courses.

"Good lesson plan and student guide"

"Content organization and presentation of the information is outstanding"

"The training was well worth the time invested"

FY11 Priority:
Develop and implement a coordinated cybersecurity strategy across DSS and support industry in its efforts to deter cyberattacks

DSS is committed to a collaborative and coherent corporate-wide strategy to combat the cyber threat to our cleared industry partners and to its own mission and capabilities. To address this cyber threat, DSS established a Cyber Security Division to mitigate the agency's collective risk through cyber vulnerability reduction and threat identification. The new office will build upon the work of the DSS Cyber Task Force, started in 2010 to align DSS and its NISP policies and procedures to best support the Department's cyber security objectives.

Cleared industry has already made great strides in understanding and mitigating the cyber threat. Cyber incident reporting to DSS has increased by 76% in FY11 with a total of 787 actionable reports received from Industry. The DSS CI Directorate relies on industry reporting, as well as other sources, to develop cyber threat awareness products including classified and unclassified editions of cyber alerts, technology and system targeting analysis, threat indicators, and specialized reports.

Additionally, information reported under the Defense Industrial Base Cyber Security/ Information Assurance cyber threat sharing program is used to inform CI risk management, analysis and reporting on the consequence of that threat to the cleared industry. DSS has maintained a 30-day turn-around for certification and accreditation of cleared contractor computer systems supporting the program's classified cyber threat sharing, assuring availability of the information.

To truly mitigate the risk posed by cyber intrusions, continued, and more robust, collaboration with other government agencies, DoD agencies and Industry is a must. DSS will continue to seek greater threat awareness and capacity in cleared industry.

FY11 Priority:
Continue timely resolution of FOCI cases and provide enhanced FOCI oversight and analysis

In a world of increasing globalization, FOCI in a cleared company is complex and not always easy to trace. Therefore, effective oversight of companies under FOCI, without hindering foreign investment, continues as a priority for DSS.

In order to better educate the NISP community and its inherent risks and challenges, DSS launched an "Understanding FOCI" web-based course to introduce important FOCI terms and processes as they relate to the NISP. The course describes the four major components of the FOCI process: identification, adjudication, mitigation, and assessment. The course explains National Interest Determinations (NIDs) and the Committee on Foreign Investment in the United States (CFIUS), and addresses aspects of foreign ownership impact on U.S. interests. The course is open to DSS, industry, and other government agency personnel involved in the FOCI process.

The Assessments and Evaluation Division implemented a system to monitor changed conditions within the NISP. The division reviews and monitors company financial data to verify self-reported financial information. It also validates financial and ownership information through a variety of open source and proprietary database research and identifies complex financial instruments that may affect FOCI thresholds. To date, the system has identified 175 changed conditions and 33 facilities under FOCI that had not been previously identified. The facilities identified with FOCI had foreign ownership ranging from five to 24 percent.

Before a company receives a facility clearance and enters the NISP, the FOCI Analytic Division conducts an extensive review of all available classified and unclassified information in order to validate self-reported FOCI and identify any unreported FOCI. Complete mitigation information related to the facilities is placed in a repository of FOCI data. The data is used to create an annual publication that presents a summary of foreign involvement within the NISP. The division also publishes *NISP in the NEWS*, a weekly summary of open source information related to NISP facilities.

The FOCI Operations Division emphasized case processing timeliness during the past year and ended the year with an average processing time of 115 days against a DSS goal of 120 days. Reduced processing time ensures FOCI mitigation instruments are emplaced in a timely manner and minimizes the risk to classified information and processes.

FY11 Priority:
Establish an Insider Threat Program within DSS

Insider: Any person with authorized access (by virtue of statutory, regulatory, or contractual authority or any other person who has been granted access) to any U.S. government resources to include personnel, facilities, information, equipment, networks, systems and operations. An insider could also include family members, friends, or associates who have access to resources by virtue of their relationship to an employee or contractor of the agency.

Insider Threat: The threat that an insider will, by acts of commission or omission, intentionally or unintentionally use their authorized access to do harm to the security of the United States. Threats can include damage to the United States through espionage, terrorism, unauthorized disclosure of information, or through the loss or degradation of departmental resources or capabilities.

During the past year, DSS took concrete steps to establish an Insider Threat Identification and Mitigation Program and Insider Threat Executive Advisory Group to manage the program. It also participated in the National Insider Threat Working Group and the DoD Insider Threat Working Group.

The DSS Insider Threat Working Group is comprised of employees from across the agency (counterintelligence, security, and information assurance) who meet to review and consider potential insider threat-related incidents and foundational process activities. The working group developed a concept of operations for an Insider Threat Program; established metrics to track insider threat risk and mitigation outcomes; defined standard operating procedures that align key DSS stakeholders; and, embarked on a strategy to acquire commercial insider threat products.

The concept of operations defines specific policies and directives for the mitigation of insider threats and fosters a collaborative environment between the three primary internal offices involved in the program.

The next steps for the program include implementing the concept of operations and standard operating procedures, tracking metrics, and purchasing and deploying Insider Threat automation products.

FY11 Priority:
Complete BRAC-mandated moves to Marine Corps Base Quantico, Va., and Fort George G. Meade, Md., with no degradation of service

The Base Realignment and Closure, or BRAC, is the congressionally authorized process DoD has used to reorganize its basing structure to more efficiently and effectively support its military forces, increase operational readiness and facilitate new ways of doing business.

As a part of the 2005 BRAC Committee recommendations, DSS, along with the Defense Intelligence Agency's Defense Counterintelligence and Human Intelligence Center (formerly the Counterintelligence Field Activity) and the three Military Department Investigative Agencies were relocated to Marine Corps Base Quantico, Va.

Under a separate BRAC recommendation, the Defense Industrial Security Clearance Office (DISCO) relocated from Columbus, Ohio, to Fort George G. Meade, Md., along with the Defense and Military Department Adjudication Facilities.

DSS was required to complete the moves by Sept. 15, 2011. The Fort Meade and Quantico moves were completed on time and under budget. As a result of a carefully choreographed process, DSS did not lose one single piece of equipment or box of documents. There were no security incidents, very few incidents of damage, but most importantly no loss of service or responsiveness to DSS customers.

Photo: Defense Adjudication Activities Facility

DISCO Relocation

For DISCO personnel, BRAC meant uprooting families and a major relocation. As a result, most DISCO employees opted not to relocate and almost 80 percent of the DISCO adjudicator workforce has been replaced in the past two years. A ceremony marking the closing of DISCO operations in Ohio was held in July and provided an opportunity to publicly honor the contributions and dedication of the DISCO work force.

Distinguished guests at the ceremony included Mayor John Wolff of Whitehall, Ohio, and representatives from the offices of Ohio Governor John Kasich, Senators Rob Portman and Sherrod Brown, and several Congressional districts. Guest speakers expressed appreciation for DISCO employees' dedication to Federal service, and recognized DISCO's long history — more than 45 years — in the Columbus metropolitan area.

Fort Meade Ribbon Cutting

A ribbon cutting for the new Adjudication Facility at Fort Meade, Md., was held in August. With the completion of the project, almost 800 employees from 14 locations are now located under one roof.

The theme of the ceremony was "the opportunity for collaboration and efficiencies to be gained from collocation." One speaker stated that the building provided a framework for the future and an opportunity to look at mission overlaps and efficiencies. Another called the 2005 BRAC recommendations "transformational" and designed to bring people together to do things better.

Russell-Knox Ribbon Cutting

A similar ceremony was held in September on Marine Corps Base Quantico to mark the successful completion of the Russell-Knox Building. The building houses approximately 2,700 employees of five activities.

The building is named for two individuals who were pioneers in creating a modern counterintelligence arm in the Department of the Navy – Marine Corps Major General John H. Russell, Jr., and Navy Commodore Dudley Knox. Both were assigned to the Office of Naval Intelligence where they joined forces to develop a capability within the Navy to conduct investigations.

In addition to the BRAC moves, DSS successfully moved 21 field locations to newer and/or larger space. The moves provide better working conditions for DSS employees.

FY11 Priority:
Continue development and implementation of the DoD Security Professional Education Development (SPeD) Certification Program

The Security Professional Education Development (SPēD) Program is the DoD strategy to professionalize the security workforce. The program was developed by the DoD security community through the DoD Security Training Council (DSTC). Chaired by DSS, the DSTC is an advisory body that provides advice and recommendations to the DSS Director and the Under Secretary of Defense for Intelligence. DSTC members helped draft the DoD 3305.13-M (DoD Security Accreditation and Certification Manual), provide subject matter experts for the development of skill standards and assessment instruments, participated in numerous working groups to develop the certification framework and operational policies, and promoted the SPeD Certification Program across DoD.

During the past year, the DSTC facilitated several landmark events and actions that included: establishing the "cut" score for the first SPeD certification, finalizing the DoD 3305.13 manual, coordinating participation for SPeD certification beta tests, and establishing implementation procedures.

The SPēD Program is divided into four core certifications:

Security Fundamentals Professional Certification (SFPC):	The individual understands foundational security concepts, principles, and practices.
Security Asset Protection Professional Certification (SAPPC):	The individual applies foundational security concepts, principles, and practices.
Security Program Integration Professional Certification (SPIPC):	The individual understands and applies risk assessment and security program management based on security concepts, principles, and practices.
Security Enterprise Professional Certification (SEPC):	The individual understands and applies concepts, principles, and practices for managing enterprise-wide security.

To obtain the SFPC, an individual must pass the assessment exam and be identified as in good standing by their component or employing organization.

Since its beta test launch in 2010, 1,633 DoD security professionals have taken the SFPC. Of that number, 708 achieved a passing score during FY11. Three conferral ceremonies were held in April 2011 that recognized the first participants. The ceremonies were held by DSS, the United States Air Force (USAF), and a combined ceremony for DoD agencies. The combined ceremony recognized individuals from DSS; DoD Office of Inspector General; Defense Threat Reduction Agency; National Geospatial-Intelligence Agency; Office of the Secretary of Defense (OSD), Office of the Deputy Under Secretary of Defense for Intelligence; Office of the DoD General Counsel; Office of the Director, Operational Test and Evaluation; Pentagon Force Protection Agency; U.S. Air Force; and Washington Headquarters Services. The Department of the Army and the Department of the Navy held similar ceremonies later in the year.

As the fiscal year ended, SFPC testing continued across DoD and beginning in FY12, SFPC testing events will be offered in conjunction with a majority of the DSS training courses.

The SAPPC beta test was launched at the DoD Worldwide Security Conference in August, 2011 and concluded in November. Upon review of the beta test results, DSS anticipates the launch of the SAPPC during the second quarter of FY12.

Certification for Adjudicators

The DoD Personnel Adjudicator Certification Program (ACP) is a specialty certification within the SPēD Certification Program. ACP identifies an adjudicator as qualified to perform all essential adjudicative tasks related to determining the eligibility of a government employee, military service member, or Defense contractor employee for access to classified information or for a position of trust. A candidate for the ACP must be a DoD Personnel Security Adjudicator at an approved DoD Central Adjudication Facility. The candidate also must meet the training, experience, and testing requirements for certification.

At the end of FY11, 251 adjudicators have taken the certification exam with 182 achieving a passing score. Once certified, adjudicators who perform due process actions may qualify for the additional credential of the Due Process assessment. Of those who passed the original assessments, six have taken and passed the Due Process assessment.

FY11 Priority:
Expand tailored assessment program to freight forwarders and Arms, Ammunition, & Explosives (AA&E) facilities

DSS began tailored assessments in 2010 to create a more efficient security review process and ensure resources were appropriately applied. The new process was first applied to facilities under FOCI as FOCI oversight is complex and a tailored approach would result in a more thorough, relevant review. This tailored approach doesn't supplant the normal DSS review, but rather supplements and enhances it based on the type of facility under review.

"The Corporate Wide Assessment has been a positive experience. It allows the senior leadership of the company to have an overall perspective of the performance of our cleared sites, identification of any trends in findings, and leveraging best practices across our enterprise. The report also enhances the message to the site leadership that their performance is being measured as a part of the whole."

"Corporate wide 'group' DSS assessments promote uniformity and consistent standards of performance across all sites. The grouping method provides clear visibility at DSS Headquarters that the company's corporate-driven security program is viable and effective, even more essential to a FOCI company where the effectiveness of a single mitigation instrument applies to all cleared facilities within the organization. Our corporate team is able to interface with a core group at DSS HQ who is 'quarterbacking' the inspections, which fosters a spirit of teamwork and adds transparency to the group inspection process. Since moving to a corporate-wide assessment format, our annual compliance ratings have risen across 90% of our cleared facilities, directly contributing to the further safeguarding of our nation's warfighters."

During FY11, DSS expanded this program to include freight forwarders and trusted foundry facilities. While these facilities constitute a very small percentage of the more than 13,000 cleared facilities, they each present a unique set of challenges. Additionally, because they constitute a small percentage of the total number of facilities, DSS personnel do not routinely encounter them. Thus, a tailored assessment with templates and a step-by-step review process serves as a refresher for DSS personnel and helps them better prepare for an upcoming review.

Freight forwarders add another layer of complexity as these companies routinely deal with foreign governments, materials and regulations.

In the case of trusted foundries, DSS developed an operations plan to explain procedures and details to focus on during a review. DSS also worked with the Defense Microelectronics Activity (DMEA) on this process. The tailored approach is designed to address DSS and DMEA interests at the facilities and ensure security practices are in place. DSS also teams with DMEA to conduct "joint" assessments of trusted foundry facilities.

Building on this momentum, DSS plans to develop a tailored assessment process for arms, ammunition and explosive (AA&E) facilities.

FY11 Priority:

Develop a procedure to standardize the security rating process nationwide in order to reduce subjectivity and increase consistency

In August 2011, DSS launched a newly designed security rating process to determine ratings assigned at the conclusion of a DSS assessment. The phased implementation began in the Capital Region, followed by the Northern Region in September and the Southern and Western Regions in October. The phased approach allowed time to train Industrial Security field personnel on the new system and incorporate industry comments or suggestions.

Security Rating Calculation Worksheet

Rating Calculation *(Complete areas in yellow)*

Note: For rating calculation purposes, treat multiple occurrences under the same NISPOM reference as one finding

Place or select "X" for each enhancement that applies to the program.

	Select CAT:	Select Category		
	Starting Score →		700	
NISP Enhancement	0			Red Flags
Category 1: Security Education (Events)				Yes/No?
Category 2: Security Education (Products)				
Category 3: Security Education (Staff Training)				
Category 4: Security Education (Community Information Sharing)				
Category 5: Self Inspection				
Category 6: Class Material Control				
Category 7: CI				
Category 8: Information Systems				
Category 9: FOCI				
Category 10: International				
Category 11: Community Membership				
Category 12: (?) Active Participation				
Category 13: Personnel Security				
Admin. Findings by Reference*				
Serious Findings by Reference*				
	FINAL SCORE →			
	Rating:	Pending		

599 & Below	=	Unsatisfactory
600 - 649	=	Marginal
650 - 749	=	Satisfactory
750 - 799	=	Commendable
800 & Above	=	Superior

DSS recognizes the importance of a consistent, objective approach to issuing security ratings as part of its security oversight role. The new security rating process uses a calculation worksheet designed to standardize and improve consistency during the rating process. It is numerically based, quantifiable, and accounts for all aspects of a facility's involvement in the NISP. Each facility begins with the same starting score – 700. 'Points' are then deducted for each security vulnerability, or added for each security enhancement and a final score is achieved. In calculating the final score, the matrix considers the size and complexity of the facility.

The rating matrix clearly separates and defines different levels of vulnerabilities. A vulnerability is defined as non-compliance with a NISPOM requirement that does not place classified information at risk to loss or compromise. A critical vulnerability, on the other hand, is defined as non-compliance with a NISPOM requirement that may place or has placed classified information at risk to loss or compromise. Once a vulnerability is determined to be serious or critical, it is further categorized as either isolated, systemic, or repeat.

An isolated vulnerability finding is a single occurrence that resulted in or could logically lead to the loss or compromise of classified information. A systemic vulnerability is a specific requirement that is deficient in multiple areas as a result of a lack of an established process, or an existing process is not adequately designed for compliance. Finally, a repeat vulnerability is a repeat of a specific occurrence identified during the last review that has not been properly corrected.

An enhancement directly relates to and enhances the protection of classified information beyond baseline NISPOM standards. Items documented as 'NISP enhancements' must relate directly to the NISP, and do not include other commonplace security measures or best practices. NISP enhancements must be validated during the assessment as having an effective impact on the overall security program. This is usually accomplished through employee interviews and review of processes/procedures.

DSS personnel will release the completed worksheet at the completion of the assessment process. Full transparency on how DSS arrived at a rating will be provided. The security rating of record will be discussed with the FSO and senior management official during the exit briefing.

DSS has established detailed guidance to field personnel on the application and use of the tool. Field personnel are also receiving training on how to complete the rating and DSS has established a process to internally share, validate, and assess the effectiveness of the tool to ensure a consistent application, on an on-going basis.

"We completed training of approximately 200 facility security officers (FSO) and alternates. It went very well and there was a very positive feel to the feedback from our FSO's about the new Matrix. We have had three or four locations undergo reviews under the new matrix - they seem pretty upbeat so far."

"This is a step in the right direction!"

"Our FSO stated that this new rating system is going to be good for her because she just received a COMMENDABLE, a first based upon four of the categories rated. She had always been told in the past she could not receive anything higher than a SATISFACTORY because her facility was not complex enough. This is now a more objective approach!"

FY11 Priority:
Reestablish an overseas industrial security presence

In June 2011, U.S. European Command (EUCOM) and U.S. Africa Command (AFRICOM) approved a DSS proposal to begin re-establishing initial industrial security operating capability within their areas of responsibility. As a result of this agreement, DSS sent a team to Stuttgart, Germany, in September to start advice and assistance meetings and assessments of eight contractor visitor groups assigned to EUCOM and AFRICOM Headquarters. Cleared contractors operating on U.S. installations overseas are not permitted to possess classified information and are not permitted to hold a NISP facility clearance. They are considered visitor groups and part of a U.S. cleared facility for which DSS currently has industrial security oversight.

The primary focus of the visit was to provide NISP education to the contractor visitor groups. Six visitor groups received satisfactory ratings and two visitor groups received commendable ratings.

The mission provided an opportunity to develop lessons learned and perfect procedures for future visits that will be scheduled based on available resources and manpower.

FY11 Priority:
Continue integration of counterintelligence into all aspects of DSS operations

DSS has made great strides in more fully integrating CI into the daily operations of the agency. Perhaps the most concrete example of this integration was the establishment of the Operations Analysis Group (OAG) in July 2010. The OAG was designed to facilitate information sharing across DSS and ensure consistent access to resources and reporting. It meets daily to orchestrate immediate DSS action on matters affecting cleared contractors under the NISP, identify and task for resolution issues that hinder effective execution of responsibilities under the NISP and ensure DSS information disseminated to law enforcement and intelligence communities is timely, effective, and complete.

Since its inception, OAG has identified a number of trends that contribute to increased risk to classified information and programs:

- Inconsistent/late reporting of suspicious contacts and security incident processing

- Exercising Dual Citizenship privileges: Individuals traveling to countries of origin and FSO not submitting incident reports/ notifying DSS.

- Country of Origin cards: Allow entry to home country on their origin card without knowledge of the U.S. Government.

- Uncleared Key Management Personnel (KMPs) resulting in invalidations

- Overdue Periodic Reinvestigation

- Foreign visitors: Maintain an accurate foreign visitor log and notify DSS of foreign visitors as soon as company accepts the visit request.

DSS CI also provides expert threat awareness training to cleared industry with the specific goal of thwarting the enemy and identifying known and suspected foreign intelligence penetrations of cleared industry. During the past year, CI provided on-site expertise to Industrial Security Field Operations, to include assessment support; review of security vulnerabilities for potential espionage indicators; and security education. CI also provided expertise to the Personnel Security adjudicative process. CI provides direct support to industry in the form of intelligence products on foreign collection targeting of industry and other finished tailored products designed to raise awareness. Internally, CI hosts guest speakers from the CI community and criminal investigators who have worked DSS-initiated cases, and presents special-topic briefings to DSS headquarters support staff to increase their awareness of the CI mission and how it supports the NISP mission.

This integration is also evident in enhanced relationships with external law enforcement and counterintelligence operations. CI works closely with federal and military CI organizations to ensure suspicious attempts to acquire restricted or classified industry technologies are investigated and the threats neutralized.

Robert "Bear" Bryant, former National Counterintelligence Executive, stressed the importance of the DSS CI capability in his summary of the 2011 Annual Counterintelligence Review of all U.S. government CI programs, stating, "The future of U.S. national security is located in the facilities and IT networks of cleared defense contractors; these assets are undoubtedly high on the target list of many foreign intelligence services. I consider DSS to be critical to our national security and, as such, I believe it imperative that it has an effective CI program..."

Other Successes and Achievements

DSS Courses Win Awards

The DSS web-based course, "Thwarting the Enemy: Providing Counterintelligence and Threat Awareness to the Defense Industrial Base," was selected as a winner of the 2010 DoD Counterintelligence and Human Intelligence Awards in the Training Education (Team) category. This award recognizes exceptional achievement related to training or educating the CI community and is sponsored by the Defense Intelligence Agency. The course provides awareness of the potential threats directed against U.S. technologies, examples of common suspicious activities, and emphasizes reporting requirements. The course was the result of close collaboration between the CI Directorate and the Center for Development of Security Excellence. The course has been very well received since it was launched in December 2010 with more than 30,000 completions to date.

The "Thwarting the Enemy" course won a second award for CDSE and their contractor support team. "Thwarting the Enemy" and the "Storage Containers and Facilities Virtual Exercise" both won a 2010 Silver Horizon Interactive Award. "Thwarting the Enemy" won in both government and educational product categories, and "Storage Containers and Facilities Virtual Exercise" won in the government category.

The Horizon Interactive Awards were created to recognize excellence in interactive media production worldwide. The judging process involves a Horizon Interactive Awards advisory panel, an end-user panel, and a worldwide panel of judges consisting of industry professionals. Winning entries are dubbed the "best of the best" in the interactive media industry.

CDSE also received Bronze Omni Awards in the government category for outstanding media production in support of two courses: "Integrating Counterintelligence and Threat Awareness into your Security Program" and "Introduction to DoD Personnel Security Adjudications." Additionally, in the education and government category, CDSE received a Silver Omni Award for "Storage Container and Facilities Practical Exercise" and a Bronze Omni Award for "Special Access Program (SAP) Overview."

The Omni Awards recognize outstanding media productions that engage, empower and enlighten. Entries are accepted in the fields of film, TV, video, interactive, animation and web. This is the third consecutive year that CDSE/Defense Security Service Academy and Carney (the support contractor) have won an Omni.

First European Security Conference and SPēD Sessions Held in Germany

The 2011 DoD European Security Conference and Security Professional Education Development (SPēD) Sessions held in Garmisch-Partenkirchen, Germany, in May 2011, not only built on the success of the 2010 DoD Worldwide Security Conference, but also took the training directly to the audience.

Conference attendees included 112 European-based DoD security professionals (military, civilian, and contractors who provide onsite security support for various DoD Components and activities). The theme of the conference was *Integrated Security in the European Environment*. To support this theme, the conference agenda featured 24 general and break-out sessions supported by 26 speakers. The agenda focused on defining requirements and discussing best practices, resulting in a better foundation for developing integrated security programs for a stronger tomorrow.

The SPēD Program was prominently featured at the event. For many in the European theater, it was their first opportunity to test their knowledge by taking the assessment. Eighty-five attendees completed the assessment and 57 percent achieved a passing score.

"Well-choreographed event. Took away a lot of info. Very interested in certification. Very worthwhile event."

"Great conference. I learned a lot regarding current initiatives and challenges in the security arena. I had a good 'recharge' of my batteries. It is nice to know that security professionals will soon be recognized as an educated and skilled work force and not just people who got stuck with the job."

2011 DoD Worldwide Security Conference and SPēD Sessions

DoD security professionals from across the globe converged in Lake Buena Vista, Fla., for the 2011 DoD Worldwide Security Conference & SPēD Sessions hosted by DSS in August. The conference theme was "Partnership for Global Security." Mr. Stan Sims, Director of DSS and sponsor of the conference, welcomed 484 attendees with opening remarks, followed by 41 general and breakout sessions.

In addition to attending conference sessions, 244 security professionals took advantage of the opportunity to test their knowledge in various security disciplines through the Security Fundamentals Professional Certification (SFPC) Test and the Security Asset Protection Professional Certification (SAPPC) Beta Test. This was the inaugural launch of the SAPPC Beta Test and 32 security professionals tested their knowledge. SAPPC Beta testers had to have been conferred the SFPC to be eligible to take the SAPPC Beta Test.

"Excellent overall conference. Excellent training."

"I have been very impressed with the entire conference. From the speakers and facilitators to the conference venue it has all been extremely professional. The partnering theme is very current. I hope next year it is something about dealing with change as it has been quite clear that this partnership is new and needs to have some of the realities of the actual integration addressed. Great job to CDSE and all who participated...can't wait until the next one."

First Graduate Level Course Developed at CDSE

The Education Division of CDSE held its first Curriculum Committee meeting in April 2011. The Curriculum Committee includes senior security officials from each of the Military Services and several DoD agencies. During this meeting, the Curriculum Committee reviewed and revised a list of approximately 15 graduate-level courses to be developed, which will become the core curriculum of the Education Division. Each course topic was discussed in detail and sub-topics were identified as well as information to be covered in each course. The courses will be developed during the next three to five years.

The first graduate-level course under this program, "Challenges in Analyzing and Managing Risk" was developed and beta tested in FY11. The first iteration of the course began in January 2012 and will run through May 4, 2012. This course is a comprehensive study of risk management as used by high-level officials to support decision making. The course addresses theory and DoD practices, and builds competence with decision-making methodology in dealing with imminent security threats. During the semester, students complete a series of assignments involving application of the principles to a specific mission or project at their agency. At course conclusion, students return to CDSE to present their project to senior leaders in the affected organization.

The course aligns with the skill standards of a DoD security specialist and is consistent with SPēD "Security Program Integration" and "Security Enterprise" certifications. The course design also takes into account the characteristics of a geographically-dispersed student population, and which includes security professionals working in many different types of assignments.

When fielded, the course will be open to DoD civilian and military personnel who have received the SFPC. In the future, the course may be open to others who have an affiliation with DoD and SFPC.

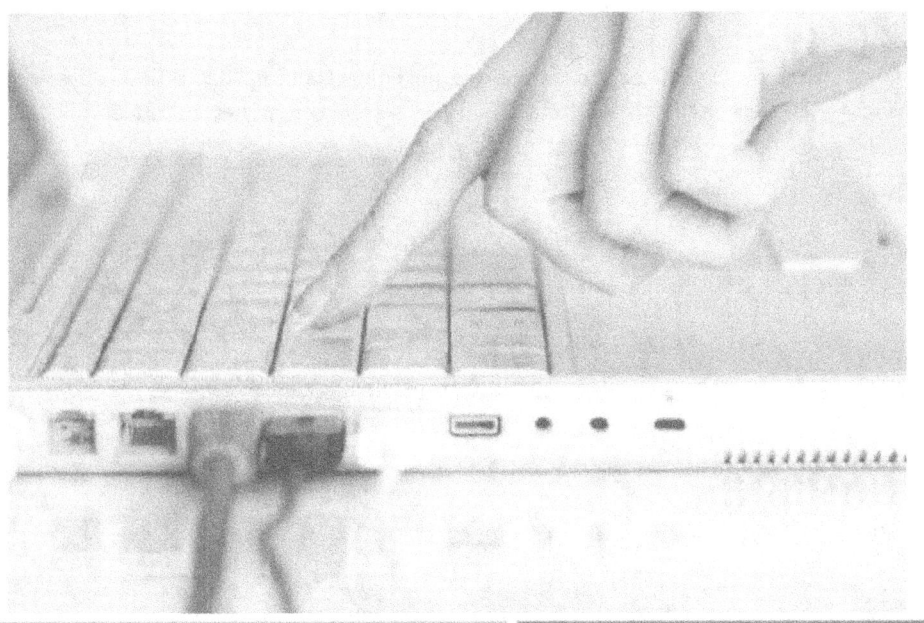

CDSE Personnel Train Iraqis

In August 2010, DSS received a request from the U.S. Embassy and U.S. Central Command (CENTCOM) J2 (Intelligence) Forward in Iraq to provide training to Iraqi personnel on the personnel security investigation and adjudication process. The request was to conduct a "train the trainer" course for personnel within the Iraqi National Security Clearance Office (NSCO), and subsequently assist trainers in delivering classes on clearance adjudications and background investigations.

This was considered critical training for the Iraq Government to develop a personnel security system to investigate, clear and vet Iraq nationals resulting in a stable government structure. In the formal request, U.S. Forces Iraq (USF-I) stated, "From our perspective, DSS is ideally suited with the type of professionals USF-I requires to conduct this vital training and fill a critical gap in Iraq's national security apparatus."

Two instructors, both military veterans, from the Center for the Development of Security Excellence (CDSE), were identified to conduct the training and travelled to Iraq in May and June 2011 to conduct the training at the NSCO in Baghdad, Iraq.

To prepare for the training, CDSE worked with J2 Forward personnel to identify a syllabus, outline a daily action plan, identify funding, define the scope of the training, select the dates of training, and details of the actions required by the host for CDSE instructors to travel to Iraq. The instructors were also required to complete Antiterrorism/ Force Protection training and received a foreign travel briefing before departure.

The training was divided into two segments. The first segment was a one-week Personnel Security Course which covered such topics as, Types and Scope of Iraqi Security Background Investigations, Agent Case Management, Supervisory Case Management, Conducting Reference Interviews, Conducting Subject Interviews, Investigative Reports, and Security Clearance Reports of Investigation. The instructors also conducted a two-week Adjudicator Course which covered the 13 Adjudicative Guidelines as well as Adjudicator Objectivity, Handling Protected Information, and Case Examples.

Forty students attended and successfully completed the training. The training created a positive link between the NSCO and CDSE, and created an interest in future U.S.-Iraq training initiatives on various security disciplines.

DSS Values:

Dependability

Respect

Integrity

Agility

Collaboration

Accountability

New Strategic Plan

DSS published a new Strategic Plan designed to guide the agency through 2016. The plan speaks to the uniqueness and importance of the agency's oversight and education missions, how DSS will ensure a responsive information technology environment to enable its mission, how the agency will retain the best and brightest, and how DSS decisions will be driven by data. Included in the Plan are the agency's updated mission, vision, values and goals.

Mission:

On behalf of the Department of Defense and other U.S. Government Departments and Agencies, the Defense Security Service supports national security and the warfighter through our security oversight and education missions. DSS oversees the protection of U.S. and foreign classified information and technologies in the hands of industry under the National Industrial Security Program (NISP) and serves as the functional manager for the DoD security professional development program. We provide security education, training, and professional development services as the functional manager for the DoD security professional development program, and for other U.S. Government personnel and contractor employees, and representatives of foreign governments, as required.

Vision:

Be the focal point of interaction and premier provider of industrial security and education services for the U.S. Government and the companies in the National Industrial Security Program in support of national security.

Values:

Our guiding principles of conduct give life to the Mission and Vision and drive organizational success. Understanding, modeling, and communicating them are daily requirements for every member of the DSS Team.

DSS by the Numbers:

13,352 active, cleared facilities in the National Industrial Security Program (NISP)

Clear and assess facilities

- 10,375 security reviews/assessments
- 1,371 new facility clearances granted
- 18,438 accredited systems in industry
- 23 Federal Partners

Adjudicate NISP Personnel Security Clearances (DISCO)

- 950,000 cleared contractor personnel
- 194,397 adjudication actions
- 24.1 days average to process 90% of initial clearances

Fund NISP Personnel Security Investigations

- Estimated $235 million expended overall in FY11
- FY12 budget request is $237 million

Mitigate Foreign Ownership Control or Influence (FOCI) in Cleared Industry

- 784 FOCI facilities
- 331 FOCI mitigation agreements
- 96 FOCI agreements emplaced FY11

Perform Counterintelligence Functions

- 19,254 Reports of suspicious contact
- 485 Investigations/operations opened due to DSS reporting
- 2,089 Intelligence Information Reports
- 30,000+ CI web-based training course completions

DoD Functional Manager for Security Training

- 200,046 course completions
- 556,725 course completions FY05 - FY11
- 45 course completions by sponsored foreign nations
- Catalog of 79 courses serving DoD and Industry
- 247% increase in course catalog since FY05

Professionalization

- 708 Security Fundamentals Professional Certifications
- 182 Adjudicator Certifications

All data is FY11 year-end data.

Cover photo: The Russell-Knox Building located at Marine Corps Base Quantico, Virginia.
The building is the new home of the Defense Security Service.

www.ingramcontent.com/pod-product-compliance
Lightning Source LLC
Chambersburg PA
CBHW080636290526
45790CB00007B/3090